Light

Contents

Revision: lower junior concepts 1-3   **2**

Concept 4   **5**
Flat, shiny things reflect light
and then we can see an image.

Concept 5   **16**
Everything reflects some light.
We see objects because they reflect
light which enters our eyes.

Checkpoint   **32**

Revision

Did you know . . . ?

★ **Very hot things are sources of light. Light travels from its source in straight lines.**

★ **Some things do not let light through. We call these things opaque. Opaque things form shadows.**

⭐ **Some things let light through.
We call these things transparent.** ▶

Task 1 Sources of light?
....

PCM 1

✦ Look at the picture.
How many different sources of light can you see?
Which things are opaque?
Which things are transparent?
Which things are translucent?
Write down your ideas.

What do you know about light?

- Start your watch. Name 12 sources of light before one minute is up.
  If you found:
  - 12 - brilliant!
  - 8 - not bad!
  - 4 - come on!
  - 0 - start again!

- Now, how many places can you think of that are completely dark?

- On a sunny day, could you go right round the outside of your school building staying in shadow all the time? How?

- Imagine a world where light could go round corners. What changes would there be?

- Think of three amazing facts you know about light. You could:
  - tell your teacher
  - tell your class
  - display them on the wall
  - write a poem about them.

⭐ Flat, shiny things reflect light and then we can see an image.

There are smooth, shiny surfaces all around us.
Smooth, shiny surfaces reflect light.
Smooth, shiny surfaces make light change direction.

All these surfaces reflect light.

A polished car gleams.

Many household gadgets shine.

Compact discs are smooth and shiny.

Shiny foods look good.

Sunglasses reflect some of the light away from our eyes.

Task 3 **Shiny Christmas**

⭐ Think about Christmas or another festival.
List all the shiny things you can think of to do with that festival.

⭐ Divide your list into light sources and light reflectors.

Task 4 Mirror maths

 There are mirrors everywhere.
How many can you spot in one day?
Start when you get up in the morning.
Only count each mirror **once**!

 Only count **one** car or you'll never
finish. How many mirrors are there on
one car?

 Record your results on a table.
Use Photocopy Master 2.

Place or object	How many mirrors?
Car	
Home	
Shop	
School	

 All mirrors reflect light.
They make light change direction.
Everything you see around you is
reflecting light.
But only mirrors make an **image** – a
picture.

Reflecting light

Look carefully at the objects you have collected.

Complete this table:

Object	Can you see your face in it?	Does it reflect light?

you need:

- a plastic mirror
- aluminium foil
- shiny plastic
- a sheet of paper
- a piece of wood
- a piece of cloth

Which of these are true?

- All objects reflect light
- All objects make an image (a picture)
- All objects reflect light; some objects make an image.

Investigating aluminium foil

 Record what you can see in a smooth, shiny piece of aluminium foil.

Now crumple the foil up a little, then smooth it out again.
What do you notice now?

It's the same foil. It's just as big, and it still reflects light. But it's not smooth any more so it doesn't reflect light like a mirror.

When the foil is flat, it reflects the light to make one picture or image.

When the foil is crumpled, it reflects the light to make many images.

◆ Now try this

Plan a magic act called, 'The Disappearing Image' using aluminium foil.

Make your plan.

Present your magic act.

Ask the others in your group what they think will happen.

Were they right?
Explain what happens.

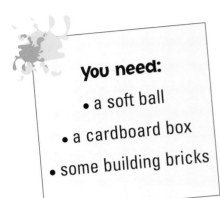

you need:

- a soft ball
- a cardboard box
- some building bricks

Bouncing balls

PCM 4

Play this game.

✶ Make a chalk mark on a smooth wall, close to the floor. This is like the smooth foil in Task 6.

✶ Roll a soft ball along the floor to bounce off the wall, close to the chalk mark.

✶ Ask a friend to hold the cardboard box to try to catch the ball in, as it rolls back from the wall. Your friend must guess where the ball will bounce back to. She must not move the box once you have rolled the ball.
What do you notice?

✶ Now make a jumbled heap of building bricks near the wall. Roll the ball towards them this time. Your friend has to guess where the ball will bounce now and catch it in the box. This is like the crumpled foil in Task 6.

✶ How does this help you to understand the way light works?

you need:
- a length of soft wood
- a wood saw
- a protractor
- a mitre block
- two plastic mirrors
- Blu-tack

Task 8 Periscope

PCM 5

 Mirrors make light change direction. You can use this to help you to see over things and round things.

 Make this periscope. You must fix the plastic mirrors to the wood at exactly 45°.

 Hold the periscope. Look in the bottom mirror. What do you see?

 Tell the story of the light's journey through the periscope. Draw pictures to help explain the story.

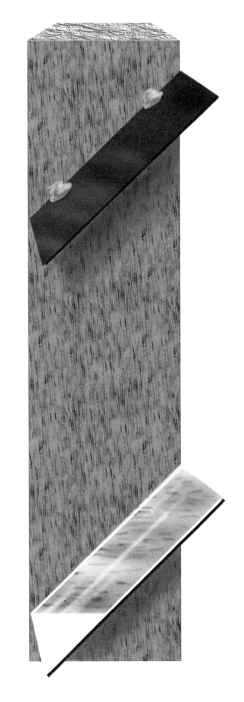

Fact File

Periscopes

Periscopes were first invented over 100 years ago, so that soldiers could look out from trenches without being seen and shot at by the enemy.

Kaleidoscope

PCM 6

- Make this kaleidoscope. Use three plastic mirrors taped together in a triangle.

- Use it to look around you. What can you see?

- Stand it on pictures and objects and look down into it. What do you notice?

Fact File

Kaleidoscopes

The first kaleidoscopes were invented in 1816 by a Scottish scientist called David Brewster. Early kaleidoscopes contained fragments of coloured glass. They were used to create **symmetrical** patterns for carpets and curtains.

Kaleidoscopes are still sometimes used today to show people what a whole room will look like when it is covered by a carpet.

Fact File

Flat mirror

Special mirrors

Look at these two car mirrors. One is flat, the other curves outwards slightly. The mirror that curves out is called a **convex** mirror. Which shows more of the road?

Convex mirror

This shaving mirror is a **concave** mirror. The mirror curves in. The image is made bigger – it is magnified.

This is a convex mirror.
Why are mirrors like this
sometimes used in shops?

This is a traffic safety mirror.
Why is it made like this?

 Task 10 Looking at a shiny spoon

- Find a shiny kitchen spoon.
  Hold the spoon up with the front
  towards you.
  Draw the image of your face.

- Hold the spoon up with the back
  towards you.
  Draw the image of your face.

- Turn the front of the spoon towards
  you again.
  Then bring the spoon close to you.
  What do you notice about the image
  of your face?

Distorting mirrors

Have you ever seen distorting mirrors at a funfair? Your image, in the mirror, is made to look very strange and **distorted**.

- Do these mirrors reflect light?
- Why are the images distorted?
  Explain what is happening to the light.

you need:

- a large plastic mirror
- thin card
- aluminium foil
- a glue stick
- a kitchen roll tube

Try bending a large plastic mirror to make your own distorting mirror.

Curve some thin card into an 'S' shape. You can curve it by pulling it gently over a table edge.
Stick a piece of smooth aluminium foil on to it.
Smooth the foil down.
Does this foil distort your image?

Stick some aluminium foil round a kitchen roll tube using a glue stick. What can you see in your cylinder mirror?

Invent some more distorting mirrors. Investigate what you see.
How many types can you make?

How could you make a model 'Hall of Mirrors' for a fairground?

 Task 12 Mirror quiz

- What do you remember about mirrors? Try this quiz.

- Look at the mirror in the photo. Explain what happens when light hits it.

- Explain how mirrors make an image. Why doesn't crumpled foil make an image?

- How would you use mirrors to look over a wall?
  Draw to show your ideas.

- How would you use mirrors to make some symmetrical patterns? Draw to show your ideas.

- Copy these three pictures.

- Draw the mirrors that are missing from the pictures.

Task 13 Black and white cat

- What do you remember about reflection of light from objects?

- If you went into a cupboard with a black and white cat and shut the door, would you see the cat?

  - Which bits would you see?
  - Would you see its white fur?
  - Would you see the cat's eyes?
  - Could you use the cat's eyes as a torch?

Draw and write to show your ideas.

Everything reflects some light. We see objects because they reflect light which enters our eyes.

Task 14 In the dark

Look at this picture. It is very dark in this tunnel. The miners can only see objects that are in the light beam from their helmet lamps. The objects reflect the light from their helmet lamps. Some of the light is reflected back into the miners' eyes.

✦ What would the miners see if they turned their lamps off but kept their eyes open?

✦ What would they see if they turned their lamps on with their eyes closed? (The objects would still be reflecting the light.)

Living without light!

✳ Find a big, safe space. Play 'Blind Man's Buff'. Now play ordinary 'Catch'. Why is it easier when we use our eyes?

✳ What will happen if this boy's torch goes out? Explain what has happened.

✳ Try this game.
Blindfold a friend. Ask him or her to build a model from LEGO.

✳ What will happen here if the candle blows out?

You need a light source to see

Stephanie, Michael and Yasmin were arguing about how you see things. They each had a different idea. They drew their ideas.

Stephanie's idea:
You see things when the light from your eye reaches them.

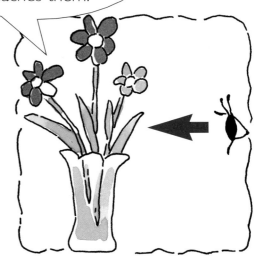

Michael's idea:
The light in the room is reflected from your eye so that you can see things.

Yasmin's idea:
The light from the flowers (and from everything else) is reflected. Some of the light enters your eyes.

If Stephanie was right, we could see in the dark!

If Michael was right we would see objects in the dark without needing to shine a torch on them – so long as a light was shining at our eyes.

🔅 Explain what you think happens.

🔅 Draw or write to show your ideas.

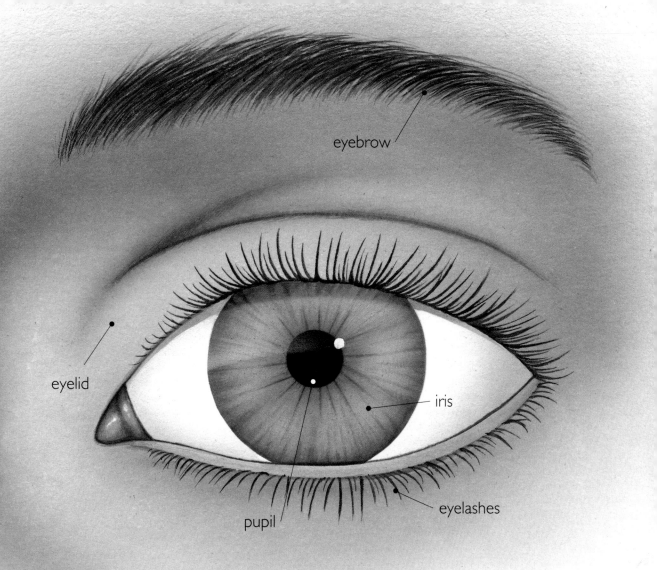

eyebrow

eyelid

iris

pupil

eyelashes

The light in your eyes

 How does light enter your eye?
Look carefully at a friend's eye.
Look for the pupil and iris.

 Use Photocopy Master 9.
Where do you think light enters
the eye?

 Ask a friend to close his eyes.
Count to 20.
Watch the very centre of his eyes as he
opens them again.
What do you notice?

Safety point:
Do not look straight
into a light source.

 Now shine a torch towards your
friend's eyes.
Don't take it too close.
Don't dazzle him.
Watch the very centre of his eyes.
What do you notice?

 Which parts of the eye seem to control
the light entering it?

Animal eyes

The eyes of all **vertebrate** animals are very similar. Remember that vertebrate animals are animals with backbones – mammals, birds, reptiles, amphibians and fish.

Owls hunt at night. The owl's pupil can be opened very wide to let in as much light as possible.

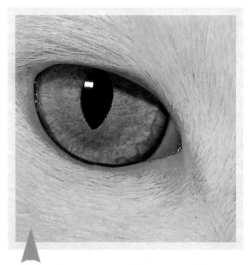

Cats hunt at night too. The shiny insides of their eyes reflect the light. The cat's eyes make the most of very little light.

The crocodile has a third eyelid. It is transparent and covers the eye when the crocodile is under water.

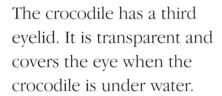

The mudskipper has eyes in two parts. One for seeing in the air, the other for seeing under water.

Fact File   A look inside your eye

There is a transparent window at the front called the cornea.

This tough coat – the white of your eye – is the strongest skin on your body!

Muscles can change the shape of your iris. They can open and close the pupil to control the light going in.

Right in the middle of the eye here is a clear jelly.

The retina lines the inside of the eye. It collects light and sends messages to the brain, except here, which is your blind spot.

Lens

These muscles pull on the lens. We can make it fat or thin!

The messages from your retina go this way, through the optic nerve to your brain.

Down here in the eyelid department, we remember to blink regularly. Blinking cleans your eyes with tears.

The image in your eye is upside-down. Your brain makes sense of the image.

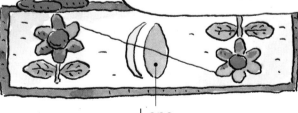

Lens

You hear through the hole in your ear. You see through a hole in your eye.

When you look at things close up, your lens goes fat to make it stronger. That focuses the light on your retina.

You use muscles to move your eye 100 000 times a day.

Complete a table about the parts of the eye and their different functions. Use Photocopy Master 10.

Task 18 Improving your eyesight

There have been many inventions for improving people's eyesight.

you need:

- a collection of lenses – both convex and concave

⭐ Look at your collection of lenses.

⭐ First, find a lens that will magnify small writing.
Light is reflected from the print and some passes through the lens and enters your eye.

Now find two lenses that you can use together to magnify the writing even more. This is a kind of microscope. Light from a window or lamp is reflected from the print, then passes through both lenses and enters your eye.

Finally, find lenses which work together to enlarge things. Try looking at a wall display. Try looking out of the window. What do you notice? This is a kind of telescope. Light is reflected from the object, then passes through both lenses and enters your eye.

Safety point:
Do not look directly at the Sun.

Find out about the people who wear glasses in your school. Use Photocopy Master 11.

Fact File

Seeing colour - cones and rods

The retina is the light-sensitive layer covering the back of your eye where the image forms. There are two sorts of light detectors in your retina – **rods** and **cones**.

Rods detect the amount of light reflected. Rods can work with very little light.

Cones detect colours. Cones need a strong light to work.

Task 19 Bedtime

- Try this at home on a dark night. Look around your bedroom before you turn out the light. How many colours can you see? You are using your cones and rods.

- Turn out the light. If it is very dark, then you may see nothing at first. But a part of your eye is expanding to take in what light there is. Do you remember which part? Keep looking.

- After a while you should be able to see things again. They may be dull and without colour. You are using your rods.

  Perhaps you think you are 'seeing in the dark'! But is your bedroom really as dark as a coal-mine? Look back to page 16.

Forming an image

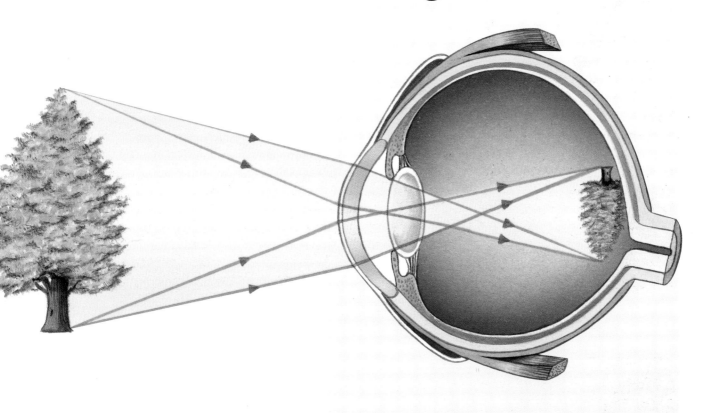

The rods and cones both react to light that falls on them. The image they send to the brain is upside down. The brain makes sense of the image so that we see it the right way up.

'Opposite' colours

Your cones can get tired. If they see too much of one colour, they tell your brain they are seeing an 'opposite' colour.

 Look hard at a piece of red paper. Stare at it for 20 seconds.

Now look quickly away at a piece of white paper.
What colour do you see?
Do you see green?

Now try some other colours.

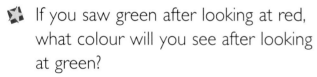

Fill in a table like this one.

Test colour	Opposite colour
Red	Green
Blue	
Yellow	
Black	

If you saw green after looking at red, what colour will you see after looking at green?
Make a **prediction** and then test your prediction.

you need:

- three bright torches
- a white screen – paper or card will do
- different coloured gels (transparent plastic sheets)
- clear tape
- a dark or shady place

✦ First, try looking around you through the coloured gels. Try single colours first, then try looking through more than one colour at a time.

blue gel

blue light

blue gel

red gel

✦ Draw or write to show your explanation of what happens.

green gel

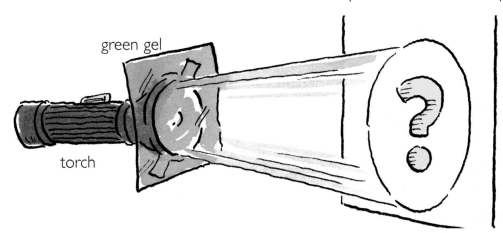

torch

yellow gel

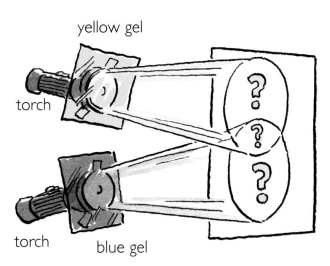

torch

torch

blue gel

✦ Now tape a piece of coloured gel to each torch. Shine the coloured light at the white screen. Draw or write to show what you think is happening.

✦ Now mix the coloured light from two torches.
Make a table to explain what happens.

27

Task 22

Which is your stronger eye?

Everyone has one eye that is stronger than the other. Which is yours?

✺ Use **both** eyes to line up a finger with the corner of the room. Keep your finger still.

✺ Close one eye. Then open it and close the other. Which way did the finger seem to 'jump'? It will jump towards your stronger eye.

Task 23

The floating sausage

Your brain puts pictures together from both your eyes. That way, it makes sense of the world. But you can fool your brain.

✺ Point with both hands. Move your fingertips together about 10 cm in front of your eyes.

✺ Look past your fingertips. What do you notice?
The 'flying sausage' is made from both your fingers.

Your blind spot

Look at the picture of the eye on page 21. Notice how the nerve comes from the back of your eye. Where that nerve comes out, you have a blind spot on the retina. You cannot pick up light that falls on to your blind spot.

✦ Draw a dot and a cross as in the picture, about 20 cm apart on a piece of paper.

✦ Close your left eye. Look at the cross. Move the paper away from you until the dot disappears.

✦ Close your right eye. Look at the dot. Move the paper away from you until the cross disappears. The light from the cross is falling on your blind spot.

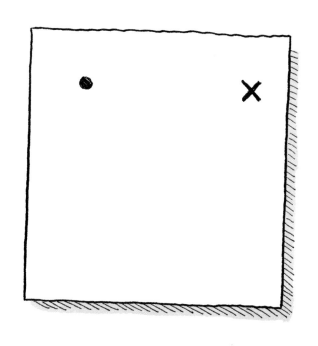

Fact File

Optical illusions

Optical illusions 'trick' you into seeing things that aren't really there. The brain is confused.

What can you see here? Is it a Christmas tree or is it something else?

◆ Now try this

Light and sound are different

✡ We see and we hear to learn more about the world around us.

✡ Complete a table like this.
Show the differences between light and sound.

Light	Sound
We see with our eyes.	We hear with our ears.
We see different colours.	We hear different sounds.

✡ How many differences did you think of? Did you think of these?

• Sound needs something – a solid, liquid or gas – to travel through. Light can travel through an empty space.

• Sound travels much slower than light. You could look in books or on CD-ROMs to find out the different speeds.

✡ Now complete a table showing how light and sound are similar.

PCM 15

- Luke and Peter are watching a cricket match from the edge of the pitch.

- Do you know why you would see the ball being hit before you hear it?

- Write an explanation. Draw pictures, too, if it helps!

That's funny. I see the batsman hit the ball before I hear it.

I think I know why.

Checkpoint

Explaining light

H G Wells wrote science-fiction stories.

In one story, 'The Country of the Blind', an explorer comes across a strange village in the mountains. The houses are plastered in a collection of strange colours. The explorer discovers that everyone in the village is blind.

 Imagine you are visiting the country of the blind. You have taken a mirror with you.

Explain to the people what a mirror is – and how it works. Use words like:

light	smooth
reflects	shiny
image	

Explain to the people how you see.

Tell them:

- why a light source is important
- how the light reflects from things
- how your eyes work.

PCM 16

Draw and write to show your ideas on Photocopy Master 16.

How can you see when the Sun isn't shining?

Do you see when beams come from your eyes?

You say light bounces off things but where does it come from?

How can this strange stuff, light, get into your body?